Wonderful World of Waffles: 60 Easy & #Delish Waffle Recipes

RHONDA BELLE

Copyright © 2016 Rhonda Belle

All rights reserved.

ISBN-13: 978-1539775201

ISBN-10: 1539775208

DEDICATION

To Foodies Everywhere...Enjoy & Be Well!

Table of Contents

Waffle Winners! 7

Amaretto Waffles 7

Apple Cinnamon Waffle Sticks 7

Apple Pie Waffles 8

Autumn Pumpkin Waffles 8

Bacon Lover's Waffles 9

Banana Belgian Beauties 9

Banana Walnut Waffles 10

Beautiful Belgian Waffles 10

Best Ever Buckwheat Waffles 11

Black Cherry Yogurt Waffle Sticks 11

Black Forest Waffles 11

Bottled Beer Waffles 12

Brownie Waffle Delight 12

Bubblin' Brown Sugar Waffles 12

Bunny Waffles 13

Buttermilk Waffles 13

Candied Yam Waffles 14

Cheesy Breakfast Waffles 14

Choco-Chip Waffles 15

Chocolate Waffles 15

Cinnamon Sugar Waffles 15

Cinnamon Swirl Waffles 16

Classic Waffles 16

Corned Beef Waffles 17

Cornmeal Waffles 17

Cranberry Citrus Waffles 17

Down Home Chicken & Waffles Sammies 18

Extra-Fluffy Spicy Sweet Waffles 18

Fig-ment of Your Imagination Waffles 19

Fresh Blueberry Beauties 19

Hammy Heartbeats 20

Hansels & Gretel Gingerbread Waffles 20

Hawaiian Island Waffles 21

Healthy Whole Grain Waffles 21

Honeyed Cornflake Waffles 22

Lemon Ginger Waffles 22

Lemon-Ricotta Waffles 23

Light & Crispy Waffles (Gluten-Free) 23

Lip-Smacking Lemonade Waffles 23

Nutty Wild Rice Waffles 24

Oatmeal Pecan Waffles 24

Over-the-Top Oat Waffles 25

Parmesan Passion Waffles 25

Peanut Butter Waffle Sticks 25

Pecan Waffles 26

Raspberry Eggnog Holiday Waffles 26

Savory Cheddar-Chive Waffles 27

Savory Herb Dinner Waffles 27

Savory Sweet Sausage Waffles 28

Strawberry French Toast Waffles 28

Sunday Cinnamon Roll Waffles 28

Super Sour Cream Waffles 29

Sweet Potato Pecan Waffles 29

Toasted Coconut Waffles 30

Vanilla Yogurt Waffles 30

Waffle Winks...Chocolate Cookies 31

Whipped Crème Waffles 31

Wonderful Walnut Maple Waffles 31

World's Easiest Waffle Sticks 32

Yummy Yeast Raised Waffles 32

BONUS: 33

Blueberry Maple Syrup 33

Homemade Honey Butter 33

ACKNOWLEDGEMENTS

To the love of my life, Johnny.
You are Mommy's greatest inspiration.

To my Mom & Dad (Sunset February 2016).
Love you always...

Waffle Winners!

Forget the expensive waffle house. Recreate the same fun experience in the comfort of your own home. Waffles are simple and easy to prepare...not to mention fun for the entire family. These 60 wonderful recipes offer a wide range of flavor combinations that will jazz up any breakfast or brunch menu. Incorporate more fruits, healthy grains, and even spices for everything from sweet to savory waffles. For best results, a waffle iron in good working condition is all you need. Try these delightful options and enjoy! Includes bonus recipes for a great homemade honey butter and also fresh blueberry maple syrup.

Amaretto Waffles

1 cup milk
1 tablespoon lemon juice
1 tablespoon sugar
1½ tablespoons imitation almond extract
2 cups all-purpose pancake and waffle mix
2 eggs
2 tablespoons baking powder

Preheat waffle maker according to manufacturer's instructions. Mix all ingredients together. Ladle batter onto waffle iron and bake until desired brownness is reached. #Delish!

Apple Cinnamon Waffle Sticks

⅓ cup vegetable oil
½ teaspoon salt
1 medium apple, grated or finely chopped
1¼ cup milk
2 cups all-purpose flour
2 eggs, separated
2 teaspoons baking powder
2 teaspoons cinnamon
3 tablespoons sugar

Preheat waffle maker according to manufacturer's instructions. In a small bowl, beat egg whites until stiff; set aside. In medium sized bowl, beat egg yolks well. Stir in milk. Add the dry ingredients to egg yolks and mix until moistened. *Take care to not overmix.* Add the vegetable oil and cinnamon; then fold in egg whites. Add apple and blend lightly; ladle batter onto waffle iron cooking surface. Bake until desired brownness is reached. #Delish!

Apple Pie Waffles

½ cup wheat bran
½ teaspoon salt
¾ cup water
1 ¾ cups whole wheat flour
1 cup skim milk
1 teaspoon apple pie spice
1 teaspoon honey
2 egg whites
2 medium apples, grated
2 teaspoons active dry yeast
3 tablespoons applesauce

In a medium bowl, stir together the flour, wheat bran, salt and apple pie spice. Set aside. In a separate bowl, stir together water and honey. Sprinkle the yeast over the surface, and let stand for about 5 minutes to dissolve. When the yeast has dissolved, stir in the apples, applesauce, milk and egg whites until well blended and then stir this mixture into the dry ingredients. Cover and let mix rest for 15 minutes. Heat the waffle iron according to manufacturer's instructions, and coat surface with cooking spray. Spoon batter onto the iron, close and cook for about 7 minutes or until the steam stops coming out and the waffle can be easily removed. Continue with remaining batter until the full batch of waffles is done. #Delish!

Autumn Pumpkin Waffles

¼ cup butter, melted
¼ cup packed brown sugar
½ teaspoon salt
1 cup canned pumpkin
1 teaspoon ground allspice
1 teaspoon ground ginger
2 ½ cups all-purpose flour
2 cups milk
2 teaspoons ground cinnamon
4 eggs, separated
4 teaspoons baking powder
APPLE CIDER SYRUP:
½ cup white sugar
1 cup apple cider
1 tablespoon cornstarch
1 tablespoon lemon juice
1 teaspoon ground cinnamon
2 tablespoons butter

Preheat waffle iron according to manufacturer's instructions. Combine the flour, baking powder, cinnamon, allspice, ginger, salt, and brown sugar in a mixing bowl. In a separate bowl, stir together the pumpkin, milk and egg yolks. Whip the egg whites in a clean dry bowl until soft peaks form. Stir the flour mixture and ¼ cup melted butter to the pumpkin mixture, stirring just to combine. Use a whisk to fold 1/3 of the egg whites into the batter. Mix gently, but well. Next, fold in the remaining egg whites. Cook waffles according to manufacturer's instructions. *To make syrup*: Stir together the sugar, cornstarch, and cinnamon in a saucepan. Stir in the apple cider and lemon juice. Cook over medium heat until mixture begins to boil; boil until the syrup thickens. Remove from heat and stir in the 2 tablespoons of butter until melted. Serve warm. #Delish!

Bacon Lover's Waffles
¼ cup butter or margarine, melted
½ teaspoon salt
1 ½ cups milk
1 ¾ cups all-purpose flour
1 pound sliced bacon
1 tablespoon sugar
2 teaspoons baking powder
3 eggs, separated
In a skillet, cook bacon until crisp. Drain; crumble and set aside. In a mixing bowl, combine the flour, sugar, baking powder and salt. Beat egg yolks, milk and butter; stir into dry ingredients until smooth. Beat egg whites until stiff peaks form; fold into batter. Add bacon. Before ladling each waffle onto the iron, stir batter. Bake waffles in a preheated waffle iron according to manufacturer's directions until golden brown. #Delish!

Banana Belgian Beauties
¼ cup butter
¼ cup whole pecans
¼ teaspoon salt
¼ teaspoon vanilla extract
½ cup pancake syrup (i.e. Mrs. Butterworth's®)
½ teaspoon ground cinnamon
¾ teaspoon baking soda
1 ½ teaspoons vanilla extract
1 1/3 cups all-purpose flour
1 1/3 cups milk
1 cup heavy cream
1 tablespoon confectioners' sugar
1/3 cup melted butter
2 teaspoons baking powder
2 teaspoons rum flavored extract
2 teaspoons vanilla extract
2 teaspoons white sugar
2/3 cup brown sugar
3 bananas, cut into half inch slices
3 eggs
Preheat a Belgium waffle iron. Whisk together the flour, baking soda, baking powder, white sugar, and salt in a bowl; set aside. Whisk together the eggs, 1 ½ teaspoons vanilla extract, and milk in a bowl. Stir in the melted butter and flour mixture until a slightly lumpy batter forms. Cook the waffles in the preheated iron until steam stops coming out of the seam, about 2 minutes. Meanwhile, melt ¼ cup of butter in a saucepan over medium heat. Stir in the brown sugar, rum extract, 2 teaspoons vanilla

extract, and cinnamon. Bring to a simmer, then stir in the pecans and continue simmering for 1 minute. Stir in the pancake syrup and bananas, continue cooking until the bananas soften, about 4 minutes. Next, beat the heavy cream, ¼ teaspoon of vanilla and confectioners' sugar with an electric mixer in a medium bowl until firm peaks form. Heat waffle iron according to the manufacturer's instructions. Once waffles are done, spoon bananas Foster sauce over waffle and top with a dollop of whip cream if desired. #Delish!

Banana Walnut Waffles

½ cup toasted, chopped walnuts
½ teaspoon baking soda
½ teaspoon kosher salt
¾ cup buttermilk
1 cup low-fat vanilla yogurt
1 cup mashed banana (2 medium bananas)
1 teaspoon baking powder
1/3 cup grapeseed or vegetable oil
2 cups unbleached, all-purpose flour
2 large eggs, lightly beaten
2 tablespoons granulated sugar

Using a whisk, combine the flour, sugar, baking powder, baking soda and salt in a large mixing bowl. Add the eggs and oil and whisk until blended. Stir in the yogurt and then the buttermilk, and whisk until mixture is smooth. Stir in banana and walnuts until incorporated. Let batter rest 5 minutes before using. Next, pour 1 ½ heaping cups of batter onto the center of a preheated waffle maker; spread batter evenly using a heatproof spatula. Let cook and then carefully remove baked waffles. Repeat with remaining batter. For best results, serve immediately. #Delish!

Beautiful Belgian Waffles

¼ cup warm milk
½ cup white sugar
¾ cup butter, melted and cooled
1 (.25 ounce) package active dry yeast
1 ½ teaspoons salt
2 ¾ cups warm milk
2 teaspoons vanilla extract
3 egg whites
3 egg yolks
4 cups all-purpose flour

In a small bowl, dissolve yeast in ¼ cup warm milk. Let stand until creamy, about 10 minutes. In a large bowl, whisk together the egg yolks, ¼ cup of the warm milk and the melted butter. Stir in the yeast mixture, sugar, salt and vanilla. Stir in the remaining 2 ½ cups milk alternately with the flour. *Be sure to end the process with flour.* Next, beat the egg whites until they form soft peaks; fold into the batter. Cover the bowl tightly with plastic wrap. Let rise in a warm place until double size. This should take about 1 hour. Preheat the waffle iron according to the manufacturer's instructions. Brush with oil and spoon onto center of iron. Close the lid and bake until it stops steaming and the waffle is golden brown. Serve immediately. #Delish!

Best Ever Buckwheat Waffles

¾ teaspoon kosher salt
1 cup buckwheat flour
1 teaspoon baking soda
1 teaspoon pure vanilla extract
2 cups unbleached, all-purpose flour
2/3 cup grapeseed or vegetable oil
3 cups buttermilk
3 large eggs, lightly beaten
3 tablespoons granulated sugar
3 tablespoons yellow cornmeal

Combine the flours, cornmeal, sugar, baking soda and salt; whisk until well blended. Add the buttermilk, eggs and vanilla. Whisk until smooth. Stir in the oil and whisk again until combined. Let batter rest 5 minutes before using. Next, pour 1 ½ heaping cups of batter onto the center of a preheated waffle maker; spread batter evenly using a heatproof spatula. Let cook and then carefully remove baked waffles. Repeat with remaining batter. Serve immediately. #Delish!

Black Cherry Yogurt Waffle Sticks

¼ cup milk
¼ teaspoon baking soda
¼ teaspoon cinnamon
½ cup black cherry yogurt
½ cup flour
½ cup pitted cherries
½ tablespoon sugar
½ teaspoon baking powder
1 egg
1 tablespoon canola oil

Preheat waffle maker according to the manufacturer's instructions. Mix yogurt, egg, sugar, oil and milk. In separate bowl, mix dry ingredients (except cherries). Add to the wet mixture and stir in. Gently fold in the fresh cherries and ladle batter onto waffle iron cooking surface. Bake until desired brownness is reached. #Delish!

Black Forest Waffles

½ teaspoon salt
1 (21 ounce) can cherry pie filling
1 ¾ cups cake flour
1 cup milk
1 cup whipping cream, whipped
1 tablespoon baking powder
2 (1 ounce) squares unsweetened baking chocolate
2 eggs, separated
3 tablespoons confectioners' sugar
3 tablespoons shortening
6 tablespoons sugar

In a mixing bowl, combine flour, sugar, baking powder and salt. Combine egg yolks and milk; stir into dry ingredients. Melt the chocolate and shortening in a microwave and add to batter; mix well. In another mixing bowl, beat egg whites until stiff peaks form; fold into the batter. Bake in a preheated waffle iron according to manufacturer's directions until browned. Combine whipped cream and confectioners' sugar. Serve waffles topped with whipped cream and pie filling. #Delish!

Bottled Beer Waffles

¼ cup milk
½ cup unsalted butter, melted
1 (12 fluid ounce) can or bottle beer
1 tablespoon honey
1 teaspoon vanilla extract
2 cups self-rising flour
2 eggs, separated

Preheat a waffle iron according to manufacturer's instructions. Combine flour, beer, butter, milk, egg yolks, honey, and vanilla in a large bowl; stir until the mixture is smooth. In a separate bowl, beat egg whites until stiff peaks form. Gently fold egg whites into batter. Spray preheated waffle iron with non-stick cooking spray. Ladle the batter into waffle iron. Cook the waffles until golden and crisp. Serve immediately. #Delish!

Brownie Waffle Delight

¼ cup unsweetened cocoa powder
¼ teaspoon salt
½ cup butter
¾ cup white sugar
1 ¼ cups all-purpose flour
1 tablespoon water
1/3 cup confectioners' sugar (decoration, optional)
2 eggs
2/3 cup chopped pecans

Preheat waffle iron according to the manufacturer's instructions. Melt butter in a sauce pan. Remove from heat and stir in cocoa. Mix in the sugar, eggs and water. Add the flour and salt, beating well. Stir in the nuts. Cook brownie in waffle iron as you would cook waffles. Sprinkle confectioners' sugar over warm waffle brownies. Serve with vanilla ice cream if desired. #Delish!

Bubblin' Brown Sugar Waffles

¼ cup brown sugar
¼ cup butter
½ teaspoon salt
1 teaspoon baking powder
1 teaspoon baking soda
2 ¼ cups all-purpose flour
2 cups buttermilk
3 egg whites
3 egg yolks

Preheat waffle iron according to the manufacturer's instructions. In a medium bowl, sift together flour, baking soda, baking powder and salt; set aside. In a large bowl, cream butter and brown sugar until light and fluffy. Beat in egg yolks. Blend in flour mixture alternately with buttermilk. In a large glass or metal mixing bowl, beat egg whites until stiff peaks form. Fold 1/3 of the whites into the batter, then quickly fold in remaining whites until no streaks remain. Spray waffle iron with non-stick cooking spray, or lightly brush with oil. Ladle the batter onto preheated waffle iron. Cook the waffles until golden and crisp. Serve immediately. #Delish!

Bunny Waffles
½ cup chopped pecans or walnuts
½ cup water
1 box carrot cake mix
2 Granny Smith apples
2 tablespoons butter
Juice of ½ lemon
Sour cream (optional)
Prepare the cake mix according to package directions, adding the chopped nuts plus up to ½ cup more water than instructed, making a thick, flowing batter. Peel, core and dice apples. Melt the butter in a sauté pan and, when it stops foaming, add the apples and toss over medium heat. Cover, lower heat and cook until soft but slightly crisp. Squeeze lemon juice over the apples. Heat the waffle iron according to the manufacturer's instructions and spray the grids with nonstick vegetable spray. Use a ¼-cup measure to pour a puddle of batter in the center of each grid. Cook the waffles until they are firm enough to remove from the waffle iron. Place on plates and spoon hot apples on top. #Delish!

Buttermilk Waffles
¾ teaspoon kosher salt
1 teaspoon baking soda
1 teaspoon pure vanilla extract
2/3 cup vegetable oil
2½ cups buttermilk
3 cups unbleached, all-purpose flour
3 large eggs, lightly beaten
3 tablespoons granulated sugar
3 tablespoons yellow cornmeal
Combine all dry ingredients in a large mixing bowl; whisk until well blended. Add the liquid ingredients and whisk until just smooth. Let batter rest 5 minutes before using. Preheat a waffle iron according to the manufacturer's instructions. Pour 1 ½ heaping cups of batter onto the center of prepared waffle iron surface; spread batter evenly using a heatproof spatula. Let cook and then carefully remove baked waffles. Repeat with remaining batter. Serve immediately. #Delish!

Candied Yam Waffles

¼ cup butter, melted
¼ cup hard packed brown sugar
¼ teaspoon freshly grated nutmeg
½ cup whole wheat flour
½ teaspoon cinnamon
½ teaspoon salt
1 ½ cups all-purpose flour
1 cup low-fat milk
1 large egg, beaten
1 tablespoon baking powder
2 medium sweet potatoes
2 teaspoons freshly grated orange peel
6 egg whites

Prick sweet potatoes several times with a fork. Microwave on high for 6 to 10 minutes until very tender and a knife goes through them easily. Cool for 10 minutes. Next, split each sweet potato in half and spoon the flesh of each into a large bowl. Discard skins. Mash the sweet potato up with a fork. Add the milk, beaten egg, brown sugar, melted butter and orange zest to the yams. Stir well to combine. In a separate large bowl, sift together the flours, baking powder, salt, cinnamon and nutmeg. Add the sweet potato mixture to the dry ingredients and stir until just combined and moistened. In a large glass or metal bowl, beat the egg whites with an electric beater until stiff peaks form. Gently, fold the egg whites into the batter. Cook per waffle maker instructions for about 5 minutes until golden. Serve hot. #Delish!

Cheesy Breakfast Waffles

¼ cup milk, or as needed
¼ cup vegetable oil
½ pound thinly sliced bacon
½ teaspoon salt
1 (1 pound) loaf processed cheese, cubed
1 ¾ cups milk
1 cup all-purpose flour
1 cup cornmeal
1 tablespoon sugar
2 ½ teaspoons baking powder
2 eggs

Preheat waffle iron according to the manufacturer's instructions. In a small bowl, mix together the eggs, milk and oil. In a larger bowl, stir together the flour, cornmeal, baking powder, sugar and salt. Make a well in the center, and pour in the milk mixture. Stir until well blended. Pour ¼ cup batter onto the heated waffle iron. Place a strip of raw bacon over the batter across each section of the waffle iron. Close the lid, and cook until steam dissipates, and the waffle is golden brown. *For the cheese sauce*: Melt processed cheese in a bowl in microwave. Gradually stir in milk until desired thickness is achieved. Drizzle cheese sauce over waffles before serving. #Delish!

Choco-Chip Waffles

½ cup vegetable oil
½ teaspoon salt
1 ¾ all-purpose cups flour
1 ¾ cups milk
1 tablespoon sugar
2 cups chocolate chips
2 teaspoons baking powder
3 egg whites, beaten stiffly
3 egg yolks, beaten

Mix all dry ingredients. Add chocolate chips. Combine yolks and milk. Stir into dry ingredients. Stir in oil and mix. Slowly fold in beaten egg whites until just mixed. Pour about ½ cup at a time into prepared waffle iron and bake until the desired brown is reached. #Delish!

Chocolate Waffles

¼ teaspoon salt
½ cup milk
1 ½ cups all-purpose flour
1 cup butter, softened
1 cup white sugar
1 teaspoon vanilla extract
2 (1 ounce) semisweet baking chocolate squares
2 eggs
2 teaspoons baking powder

In a microwave-safe bowl, microwave chocolate until melted. Stir until smooth. Set aside. In another bowl, mix the butter and sugar. Add the eggs one at a time, beating well after each one. Stir in chocolate and vanilla. In a separate bowl, combine flour, baking powder, and salt; add gradually to the butter and sugar mixture, alternating with the milk. Spray preheated waffle iron with non-stick cooking spray. Pour mix onto hot waffle iron. Cook until crisp and serve hot with favorite syrup. #Delish!

Cinnamon Sugar Waffles

¼ cup packed light or dark brown sugar
¾ teaspoon kosher salt
1 tablespoon ground cinnamon
1 teaspoon baking soda
1 teaspoon pure vanilla extract
2/3 cup vegetable oil
2 ½ cups buttermilk
3 cups unbleached, all-purpose flour
3 large eggs, lightly beaten
3 tablespoons yellow cornmeal

Combine the flour, cornmeal, sugar, baking soda, salt and cinnamon in a large mixing bowl; whisk to blend. Add the buttermilk, eggs, vanilla and the oil. Whisk until well blended and smooth. Let batter rest 5 minutes. Pour 1 ½ heaping cups of batter onto the center of a preheated waffle maker; spread batter evenly using a heatproof spatula.

Let cook and then carefully remove baked waffles. Repeat with remaining batter. Serve immediately. #Delish!

Cinnamon Swirl Waffles

¼ cup butter, melted
¼ teaspoon salt
½ tablespoon white sugar
½ teaspoon baking soda
1 ½ teaspoons baking powder
1 cup all-purpose flour
1 cup buttermilk
1 pinch ground cinnamon
1 teaspoon vanilla extract
2 egg whites
2 egg yolks

Preheat your waffle iron according to the manufacturer's instructions. In a medium bowl, whisk together the eggs, vanilla, buttermilk and butter until well blended. Combine the flour, baking powder, baking soda, sugar, salt and cinnamon; stir into the buttermilk mixture. In a separate bowl, whip the egg whites with an electric mixer until stiff. Fold into the batter. Spoon batter onto the hot waffle iron, close, and cook until golden brown. Waffles are usually done when steam disappears. #Delish!

Classic Waffles

1 ½ cups warm milk
1 teaspoon salt
1 teaspoon vanilla extract
1/3 cup butter, melted
2 cups all-purpose flour
2 eggs
2 tablespoons white sugar
4 teaspoons baking powder

In a large bowl, mix together flour, salt, baking powder and sugar; set aside. Preheat waffle iron to desired temperature. In a separate bowl, beat the eggs. Stir in the milk, butter and vanilla. Pour the milk mixture into the flour mixture; beat until blended. Ladle the batter into the preheated waffle iron. Cook waffles until golden and crisp. Serve immediately. #Delish!

Corned Beef Waffles

½ (12 ounce) can corned beef, broken into pieces
1 ¼ cups milk
1 ½ cups all-purpose flour
1 pinch salt
2 eggs
2 teaspoons baking powder
2 teaspoons cooking oil

Preheat waffle iron. In a medium bowl, mix together the eggs, milk and oil. Combine the flour, salt and baking powder; stir into the milk mixture until it makes a smooth batter. Stir in corned beef. Spoon batter onto your waffle iron, close the lid, and cook until the waffle iron stops steaming and waffles are golden. Serve hot with butter. #Delish!

Cornmeal Waffles

¾ teaspoon baking soda
1 ½ cups cornmeal
1 ¾ cups nonfat buttermilk
1 cup whole wheat flour
2 ½ tablespoons white sugar
2 tablespoons baking powder
4 egg whites

Preheat a waffle iron and coat with cooking spray. In a medium bowl, stir together the whole wheat flour, cornmeal, sugar, baking powder and baking soda. Make a well in the center, and stir in the buttermilk just until smooth. In a separate bowl, whip egg whites with an electric mixer until thick enough to hold a soft peak. Carefully fold the egg whites into the batter. Spoon batter onto the hot waffle iron in an amount appropriate for your iron. Close and cook until the iron stops steaming, and the waffles are golden brown. #Delish!

Cranberry Citrus Waffles

¼ cup chopped pecans or walnuts
½ cup orange juice
½ teaspoon salt
¾ cup whole milk
1 ½ cups all-purpose flour
1 teaspoon grated orange peel
1 teaspoon vanilla
1/3 cup dried cranberries
2 large eggs
2 tablespoons sugar
3 tablespoons vegetable or canola oil
4 teaspoons baking powder

In a large mixing bowl, sift together the flour, sugar, baking powder and salt. In a separate bowl, beat the eggs with the evaporated milk, juice, oil, orange peel and vanilla. Add the wet ingredients to the dry and stir until just blended. Fold in the berries and the nuts. Bake the waffles according to your waffle maker's instructions until golden brown. #Delish!

Down Home Chicken & Waffles Sammies

¼ cup heavy cream
1 cup cornstarch
1 quart peanut oil for frying
1 tablespoon ground black pepper
1 tablespoon salt
1 tablespoon salt
2 cups all-purpose flour
2 tablespoons cayenne pepper
4 large fresh eggs
8 chicken tenders

Whisk together the eggs, cream, cayenne pepper, 1 tablespoon salt, and black pepper in a large bowl. In a paper bag, shake together the flour, cornstarch, and 1 tablespoon salt. Dip the chicken into the beaten egg mixture, then place into the flour mixture and shake to coat. Place the breaded chicken onto a wire rack; do not stack. Let the chicken rest for 20 minutes to allow the coating to set. Heat about 3" of oil in a deep-fryer or large saucepan to 375 degrees. In small batches, fry chicken 5 to 8 minutes until golden brown. Remove chicken, and drain on paper towels. Set aside or keep warm in a low oven. Combine the mayonnaise, maple syrup, horseradish, and mustard powder in a medium bowl. Place the bacon in a large, deep skillet, and cook over medium-high heat, turning occasionally, until evenly browned, about 10 minutes. Drain the bacon slices on a paper towel-lined plate. *To assemble the sandwiches*: Place 4 waffles on a cookie sheet, top each waffle with 2 chicken tenders, 3 slices of bacon, and 2 slices of cheddar. Broil the sandwich for a 3 to 5 minutes until the cheese melts. Spread 3 tablespoons of the maple mayonnaise on the remaining 4 waffles and place on top of the sandwich. #Delish!

Extra-Fluffy Spicy Sweet Waffles

¼ cup vegetable oil
½ teaspoon salt
1 tablespoon sugar
2 cups all-purpose flour
2 cups milk
2 teaspoons baking powder
3 eggs, separated
CINNAMON CREAM SYRUP:
¼ cup water
½ cup light corn syrup
½ teaspoon ground cinnamon
1 (5 ounce) can evaporated milk
1 cup sugar
1 teaspoon vanilla extract

In a bowl, combine the flour, sugar, baking powder and salt. Combine the egg yolks, milk and oil; stir into dry ingredients just until moistened. In a small mixing bowl, beat egg whites until stiff peaks form; fold into batter. Bake in a preheated waffle iron according to manufacturer's directions. *To make syrup*: Combine sugar, corn syrup and water in a saucepan. Bring to a boil over medium heat; cook and stir until thickened. Remove from the heat; stir in the milk, vanilla and cinnamon. Serve over the waffles. #Delish!

Fig-ment of Your Imagination Waffles

½ teaspoon salt
¾ cup dried figs
1 ½ cups milk
1 teaspoon grated lemon rind
2 cups sifted cake flour
2 tablespoon sugar
2 tablespoons double-acting baking powder
3 egg whites, stiffly beaten
3 egg yolks
7 tablespoons butter, melted

Allow figs to stand in boiling water for 10 minutes. Remove blossoms and stems with scissors; chop figs into small pieces. Sift flour, measure, then re-sift into mixing bowl with remaining dry ingredients. Add lemon rind and finely cut figs. Combine well-beaten egg yolks with milk and melted butter. Mix lightly into dry ingredients, then fold in stiffly beaten egg whites. Bake on hot waffle iron until golden brown. #Delish!

Fresh Blueberry Beauties

¼ cup melted butter
½ cup orange juice
½ teaspoon salt
1 ½ cups blueberries
1 2/3 cups milk
1 tablespoon cornstarch
2 ¼ teaspoons baking powder
2 cups all-purpose flour
2/3 cup fresh blueberries
3 egg whites, stiffly beaten
3 egg yolks, beaten
3 tablespoons honey

In a medium bowl, whisk together egg yolks and milk. Stir in flour, baking powder and salt. Stir in butter, and set mixture aside for about 30 minutes. Preheat a lightly greased waffle iron. Fold egg whites and 2/3 cup blueberries into the mixture. Scoop portions of the mixture into the prepared waffle iron, and cook until golden brown according to the manufacturer's instructions. *To prepare the sauce*: In a medium saucepan over medium heat, mix 1 ½ cups blueberries, honey and ¼ cup orange juice. Bring to a boil. Mix remaining orange juice and cornstarch in a small bowl, and stir into the blueberry mixture. Stir constantly until thickened. Serve warm over waffles. #Delish!

Hammy Heartbeats

½ cup finely chopped ham
½ teaspoon salt
1 ½ cups milk
2 cups sifted flour
3 eggs, separated
3 teaspoons baking powder
5 tablespoons melted shortening

Mix and sift dry ingredients. Combine beaten egg yolks, milk and shortening; add to dry ingredients, beating until smooth. Stir in finely chopped ham. Fold in stiffly-beaten egg whites. Pour a spoonful of batter into each section of hot waffle iron. Bake until golden. #Delish!

Hansels & Gretel Gingerbread Waffles

¼ cup molasses
¼ teaspoon dry mustard
¼ teaspoon salt
½ teaspoon baking soda
½ teaspoon ground allspice
¾ cup buttermilk
¾ teaspoon ground cinnamon
1 ½ teaspoons baking powder
1 cup all-purpose flour
1 egg, separated
1 teaspoon ground ginger
1/3 cup chopped raisins
1/3 cup packed brown sugar
1/8 teaspoon cream of tartar
3 tablespoons butter or margarine, melted

In a bowl, combine flour, baking powder, ginger, cinnamon, allspice, baking soda, mustard and salt; set aside. In a large mixing bowl, beat brown sugar and egg yolk until fluffy. Add buttermilk, molasses and butter; stir into dry ingredients just until combined. Add raisins. In a small bowl, beat egg white and cream of tartar until soft peaks form. Gently fold into batter. Bake in a preheated waffle iron according to manufacturer's directions until golden brown. #Delish!

Hawaiian Island Waffles

¼ cup coconut milk
¼ teaspoon baking soda
¼ teaspoon salt
½ tablespoon white sugar
¾ cup chopped fresh pineapple
1 ¼ cups sifted all-purpose flour
1 cup sour cream
1 egg yolk
1 teaspoon baking powder
2 large egg whites, beaten
5 tablespoons unsalted butter, melted

Preheat a lightly greased waffle iron according to the manufacturer's instructions. In a medium bowl, sift together flour, sugar, baking powder, baking soda and salt. In a separate medium bowl, mix egg yolk, sour cream, coconut milk, pineapple and butter. Thoroughly stir in flour mixture. Gently fold in egg whites. Pour the mixture into the prepared waffle iron, and cook until golden brown and steam disappears. #Delish!

Healthy Whole Grain Waffles

¼ cup all-purpose flour
¼ cup canola oil
¼ cup unsweetened applesauce
¼ cup wheat germ
¼ teaspoon salt
½ cup flax seed meal
1 ¾ cups skim milk
1 cup whole wheat pastry flour
1 tablespoon sugar
1 teaspoon vanilla extract
2 eggs, beaten
4 teaspoons baking powder

In a large bowl, whisk together the eggs, milk, oil, applesauce, and vanilla. Beat in whole wheat pastry flour, flax seed meal, wheat germ, all-purpose flour, baking powder, sugar, and salt until batter is smooth. Preheat a waffle iron according to the manufacturer's instructions, and coat with cooking spray. Pour batter into waffle iron in batches, and cook until crisp and golden brown. #Delish!

Honeyed Cornflake Waffles

¼ teaspoon salt
½ cup vegetable oil
¾ cup crushed cornflakes
1 ¼ cups all-purpose flour
1 ¾ cups milk
1 tablespoon baking powder
2 eggs, separated
HONEY SAUCE:
¼ cup butter or margarine
½ cup maple syrup
½ teaspoon ground cinnamon
1 cup honey
1 dash ground nutmeg

In a bowl, combine flour, cornflakes, baking powder and salt. Beat egg yolks lightly; add milk and oil. Stir into dry ingredients just until combined. Beat egg whites until stiff peaks form; fold into batter. Bake in a preheated waffle iron according to manufacturer's directions until golden brown. *For honey sauce*: Combine honey, syrup, butter, cinnamon and nutmeg in a saucepan. Cook and stir on medium-low until heated through. Pour over warm, buttered waffles. #Delish!

Lemon Ginger Waffles

¼ teaspoon ground ginger
½ cup finely chopped candied/crystallized ginger
¾ teaspoon kosher salt
1 tablespoon lemon zest
1 teaspoon baking soda
1 teaspoon pure vanilla extract
2/3 cup vegetable oil
3 ½ cups unbleached, all-purpose flour
3 cups buttermilk
3 large eggs, lightly beaten
3 tablespoons granulated sugar
3 tablespoons yellow cornmeal

Combine the flour, cornmeal, sugar, baking soda, salt and ground ginger in a large mixing bowl; whisk until well blended. Stir in the zest and candied ginger. Add the liquid ingredients and whisk until just smooth. Let batter rest 5 minutes before using. Pour 1 ½ heaping cups of batter onto the center of a preheated waffle maker; spread batter evenly using a heatproof spatula. Let cook and then carefully remove baked waffles. Repeat with remaining batter. Serve immediately with butter. #Delish!

Lemon-Ricotta Waffles

½ teaspoon each almond, lemon, and vanilla extract
½ teaspoon salt
1 tablespoon baking powder
1 tablespoon sugar
1 teaspoon lemon zest (packed), plus additional for garnish
1/3 cup skim ricotta
1 ¼ cups skim milk
2 cups flour
2 eggs, lightly beaten
2 tablespoons butter
Warm maple syrup, butter and berries of choice for serving
Preheat your waffle iron according to the manufacturer's instructions and coat with nonstick cooking spray. Melt butter and set aside to cool. In a medium bowl whisk together the flour, sugar, baking powder, salt, and zest. In another medium bowl, whisk the eggs, milk, ricotta, extracts, and melted butter. Pour the wet ingredients into the dry and stir to blend. *Do not overmix.* Scoop about 1 cup of the moderately thick batter and ladle into the center of your waffle iron and cook. Serve with berries, butter, and maple syrup. #Delish!

Light & Crispy Waffles (Gluten-Free)

¼ cup granulated sugar
¼ cup milk powder
½ cup grapeseed or vegetable oil
½ cup tapioca starch (flour)
1 tablespoon baking powder
1 tablespoon pure vanilla extract
1 ½ teaspoons kosher salt
2 large eggs, lightly beaten
2 ½ cups buttermilk
3 ½ cups rice flour
Combine the dry ingredients; whisk until well blended. Add the remaining ingredients and whisk until just combined. Let batter rest 5 minutes before using. Pour 1 ½ heaping cups of batter onto the center of a prehcated waffle maker; spread batter evenly using a heatproof spatula. Let cook and then carefully remove baked waffles. Repeat with remaining batter. Serve immediately. #Delish!

Lip-Smacking Lemonade Waffles

¼ cup melted butter
¼ cup sugar
½ teaspoon baking powder
½ teaspoon salt
1 ¼ cups flour
1 cup milk
1 tablespoon fresh lemon juice
4 large eggs - separated
Grated peel of one whole lemon

In a medium bowl, beat egg yolks with the sugar and salt. Blend in the milk, lemon juice, lemon peel, and butter, beating well. Add the flour and baking powder. Beat egg whites until stiff and fold into batter. Bake in a preheated waffle iron until golden brown and cover with maple syrup while warm. #Delish!

Nutty Wild Rice Waffles
¼ cup vegetable oil
½ cup chopped pecans
½ teaspoon salt
1 ½ cups cooked wild rice
1 cup all-purpose flour
1 teaspoon baking powder
2 eggs, separated
2/3 cup milk
In a bowl, combine the flour, baking powder and salt. In a mixing bowl, beat egg yolks, milk and oil; stir into dry ingredients just until moistened. In another bowl, beat egg whites until stiff peaks form; fold into batter. Fold in the rice and the pecans. Bake in a preheated greased waffle iron according to manufacturer's directions until golden brown. #Delish!

Oatmeal Pecan Waffles
¼ cup unsalted pecans, chopped
½ cup quick-cooking oats
1 ½ cup fat-free milk
1 cup whole wheat flour
1 tablespoon vegetable oil
1 teaspoon sugar
2 large eggs, separated
2 teaspoon baking powder
Preheat waffle iron according to the manufacturer's instructions. Combine flour, oats, baking powder, sugar, and pecans in a large bowl. Combine egg yolks, milk, and vegetable oil in a separate bowl, and mix well. Add liquid mixture to the dry ingredients, and stir well. *Do not overmix.* A few lumps are okay. Next, whip egg whites to medium peaks. Gently fold egg whites into batter Pour batter into preheated waffle iron, and cook until golden and/or steam stops disappears. Serve alongside fresh fruit and light dusting of powdered sugar to each waffle. #Delish!

Over-the-Top Oat Waffles

½ teaspoon salt
1 ¾ cups fat-free milk
1 cup all-purpose flour
1 cup oat flour
1 tablespoon sugar
1 teaspoon vanilla extract
2 eggs
2 tablespoons canola oil
4 teaspoons baking powder
In a bowl, combine the first five ingredients. Combine the eggs, milk, oil and vanilla; stir into dry ingredients just until combined. Pour batter by ½ cupfuls into a preheated waffle iron; bake according to manufacturer's directions until golden brown. Butter lightly. Garnish with fresh berries of the season and powdered sugar. #Delish!

Parmesan Passion Waffles

¼ cup vegetable oil
½ cup grated parmesan cheese
½ teaspoon ground rosemary (optional)
¾ cup milk
1 ¾ cups all-purpose flour
1 cup buttermilk
1 teaspoons kosher salt
2 eggs, separated
3 teaspoons baking powder
Add buttermilk, milk and oil to egg yolks. Beat together. Combine flour, baking powder and seasonings in another bowl, then fold into the egg/buttermilk mixture. Whip the egg whites into soft peaks and fold into the batter. Add parmesan last and fold to gently mix. Pour waffle batter into the hot waffle iron heated according to manufacturer's directions and cook until golden brown. #Delish!

Peanut Butter Waffle Sticks

2 tablespoons extra crunchy peanut butter
2 tablespoons regular syrup (microwaved)
6 waffle sticks, frozen and prepared according to the package or made from the World's Easiest Waffle Sticks recipe in this book
Dash ground cinnamon
Candied sprinkles of choice
Combine peanut butter, syrup, and cinnamon in small microwave- proof bowl. Microwave for 10-15 seconds. Stir to combine. Dip waffle sticks into syrup and coat with sprinkles. #Delish!

Pecan Waffles

¼ cup chopped pecans
¼ teaspoon salt
½ teaspoon maple flavoring
1 teaspoon baking soda
2 teaspoons baking powder
2 cups all-purpose flour
2 cups buttermilk
2 eggs
2 tablespoons brown sugar
3 tablespoons vegetable oil

Combine flour, brown sugar, baking powder, baking soda, and salt in a large bowl. Stir in pecans. Whisk buttermilk, eggs, oil, and maple flavoring in medium bowl. Whisk milk mixture into dry ingredients just until dry ingredients are thoroughly moistened. Preheat waffle maker. Pour 1 cup of batter onto the center of the bottom grid. Close top and flip waffle maker. Bake until golden. Remove, butter and serve hot. #Delish!

Raspberry Eggnog Holiday Waffles

1 ½ cups all-purpose flour
1 ½ cups eggnog
1 cup raspberry preserves
1 cup whipped cream, to garnish (optional)
1 egg, beaten
1 tablespoon sugar
2 ½ teaspoons baking powder
2 cups raspberries
2 tablespoons butter, melted

Heat a waffle iron according to manufacturing instructions. Mix the flour, sugar, and baking powder together in a mixing bowl. Stir in 1 cup eggnog, butter, and the egg until well blended. Add more eggnog if needed to make a pourable batter. Lightly grease or spray the waffle iron with non-stick cooking spray. Pour some batter onto the preheated waffle iron, close the top, and cook until golden brown and crisp on both sides. Serve warm with raspberry preserves drizzled over each waffle. Top with fresh whole raspberries and a dollop of whipped cream if desired. #Delish!

Savory Cheddar-Chive Waffles

¼ cup chopped fresh chives
1 cup shredded, extra-sharp cheddar
1 teaspoon baking soda
1 teaspoon kosher salt
2 tablespoons granulated sugar
2/3 cup grapeseed or vegetable oil
3 ½ cups unbleached, all-purpose flour
3 cups buttermilk
3 large eggs, lightly beaten
3 tablespoons yellow cornmeal

Combine the flour, cornmeal, sugar, baking soda and salt in a large mixing bowl; whisk to combine. Add the buttermilk, eggs and oil; whisk until just combined. Stir in the chives and Cheddar. Let batter rest 5 minutes before using. Preheat waffle iron. Pour 1½ heaping cups of batter onto the center of the lower grid of the preheated waffle maker; spread evenly using a heatproof spatula. Cook until golden. Repeat with remaining batter. For best results, butter and serve immediately. #Delish!

Savory Herb Dinner Waffles

¼ teaspoon dried tarragon
½ cup vegetable oil
½ teaspoon dried rosemary
1 ½ cups shredded smoked Gouda cheese
1 teaspoon baking soda
1 teaspoon dried parsley
1 teaspoon garlic salt
2 cups all-purpose flour
2 cups buttermilk
2 teaspoons baking powder
2/3 cup light sour cream
3 eggs, separated

In a large bowl, stir together the flour, baking powder, baking soda, garlic salt, parsley, rosemary and tarragon. Stir in the shredded Gouda. Set aside. In another bowl, mix together the egg yolks, buttermilk, sour cream and vegetable oil until well blended. Pour the wet ingredients into the flour mixture, and stir until just blended. In a separate clean bowl, whip the egg whites until stiff peaks form. Fold into the waffle batter. Heat the waffle iron, and coat with nonstick spray. Use the recommended amount of batter for each waffle according to your iron. Close the lid, and cook until golden brown. These are wonderful with beef or chicken and gravy. #Delish!

Savory Sweet Sausage Waffles

1 1/3 cups milk
1 cup applesauce
1 lb. bulk pork sausage
1 teaspoon ground cinnamon
1/8 teaspoon ground nutmeg
2 ½ cups all-purpose flour
2/3 cup vegetable oil
3 eggs, separated
4 teaspoons baking powder

In a skillet, brown and crumble sausage and cook well. Drain fat and set aside. In a large bowl, combine flour, baking powder, cinnamon and nutmeg. In another bowl, beat egg yolks lightly. Add milk, applesauce and oil; mix well. Stir into dry ingredients just until combined. Beat egg whites until stiff peaks form; fold into batter. Add drained sausage to batter. Bake in a preheated waffle iron according to manufacturer's directions until golden brown. Serve immediately. #Delish!

Strawberry French Toast Waffles

¼ cup fat-free milk
¼ cup light pancake syrup
1 cup sliced fresh strawberries
1 egg
1 egg white
4 slices whole wheat or white bread

In a shallow dish, beat the egg, egg white and milk. Dip bread into egg mixture, coating both sides. Bake in a preheated waffle iron according to manufacturer's directions until golden brown. *For sauce:* in a bowl, crush the strawberries; stir in the pancake syrup. #Delish!

Sunday Cinnamon Roll Waffles

¼ cup + 2 tablespoons unsweetened almond milk
¼ cup canned pumpkin, not pie filling
¼ tsp baking powder
½ cup whole-wheat flour
½ tsp cinnamon
½ tsp vanilla extract
1 tablespoon granulated Stevia
1 whole large egg
CREAM CHEESE ICING:
¼ cup plain nonfat Greek yogurt
1 tablespoon granulated Stevia
2 tablespoons reduced-fat cream cheese (room temperature)

Preheat waffle iron to medium heat. Mix whole-wheat flour, protein powder, Stevia, baking powder, and cinnamon in bowl. In a separate bowl, mix egg, almond milk, vanilla extract, and pumpkin. Add wet ingredients to dry and gently mix until combined. Spray waffle iron with cooking spray. Spoon batter into waffle iron to make three waffles. Cook for about 4-5 minutes or until golden brown. *For icing:* Mix room-temperature cream cheese, Greek yogurt and stevia. Spoon icing into a plastic bag or piping bag. Cut the end off and pipe frosting onto waffles. A final sprinkle of cinnamon makes a nice garnish. #Delish!

Super Sour Cream Waffles
¼ teaspoon white vinegar
½ cup plain yogurt
½ cup sour cream
½ teaspoon salt
1 cup water
1 teaspoon baking soda
2 cups all-purpose flour
2 eggs, beaten
2 teaspoons baking powder
In a bowl, mix together water, sour cream, yogurt, and vinegar. Sift flour into a separate, large bowl; stir in baking powder, baking soda, and salt. Add sour cream mixture and eggs to flour mixture; blend until smooth. Cook on a lightly greased waffle iron until golden brown. Serve buttered and hot. #Delish!

Sweet Potato Pecan Waffles
¼ cup chopped pecans
1 ½ cups cake flour
1 cup canned sweet potato puree
1 cup milk
1 tablespoon baking powder
1 tablespoon white sugar
1 teaspoon ground nutmeg
1 teaspoon salt
2 tablespoons pecans, chopped
3 egg whites
3 egg yolks
3 tablespoons butter, melted
Preheat waffle iron according to the manufacturer's instructions. Stir together flour, baking powder, sugar, salt, nutmeg, and ¼ cup pecans. Mix sweet potato puree, egg yolks, and milk in a large bowl until well combined. Add flour mixture, and mix well. Beat egg whites until stiff peaks form. Fold ¼ of the egg whites into batter. Lightly fold remaining whites and melted butter into the batter. Cook in hot waffle iron. Garnish with more chopped pecans. #Delish!

Toasted Coconut Waffles

¼ cup butter – melted
¼ teaspoon baking soda
¼ teaspoon salt
½ teaspoon coconut extract
1 ¼ cup all-purpose flour
1 ½ cup milk
1 teaspoon vanilla extract
2 teaspoons baking powder
2/3 cup shredded coconut
3 large eggs, separated
3 tablespoons sugar (optional)

Place coconut in a large frying pan over medium high heat. Stir often until coconut is lightly browned and the smell begins to float in the air. Remove from heat and set aside. Next, in large bowl, mix together the toasted coconut, flour, sugar, baking powder, baking soda and salt. In a separate bowl, beat the egg yolks with the milk, coconut extract, vanilla extract and melted butter. In yet another bowl, beat the egg whites with an electric mixer until stiff peaks form. Add the egg yolk mixture to the dry ingredients and mix well. Fold the beaten egg whites into the combined mixture. Bake waffles in your waffle iron per instructions using approximately ½ cup of batter per waffle. Serve hot with fresh fruit or whipped butter. #Delish!

Vanilla Yogurt Waffles

½ cup shortening
½ teaspoon kosher salt
1 ¼ cups all-purpose flour
1 ½ cups vanilla fat-free yogurt
1 teaspoon baking soda
2 teaspoons baking powder
3 eggs

Preheat a waffle iron according to manufacturer's instructions. Beat eggs in a large mixing bowl, then add yogurt, flour, baking powder, baking soda, kosher salt, and shortening, mixing until smooth. Pour batter onto hot waffle iron. Cook until no longer steaming, about 5 minutes. #Delish!

Waffle Winks...Chocolate Cookies

½ cup butter
½ teaspoon salt
1 ½ cups all-purpose flour
1 cup packed brown sugar
1 teaspoon baking powder
1 teaspoon vanilla extract
2 (1 ounce) unsweetened chocolate squares
2 eggs

Melt chocolate over low heat. Cream together sugar and butter or margarine. Add chocolate and mix well. Add eggs and dry ingredients. Mix well. Heat waffle iron and use nonstick spray. Cook 1 tablespoon of dough in each section of preheated iron. Bake until cookies start to turn brown. *Avoid burning.* Cool and frost with white vanilla flavored frosting. #Delish!

Whipped Crème Waffles

¼ teaspoon salt
1 cup all-purpose flour
1 cup heavy whipping cream
3 eggs, separated

In a large mixing bowl, combine flour and salt. In a small mixing bowl, beat egg yolks on low while adding cream for approximately 1 minute. Add to flour mixture; combine on low speed, then beat on medium- high until smooth. In another small mixing bowl and with clean beaters, beat egg whites on high until stiff peaks form. Gently fold into batter. Bake in a preheated waffle iron according to manufacturer's directions. Serve with warm maple syrup or fresh seasonal fruit. #Delish!

Wonderful Walnut Maple Waffles

¼ cup maple syrup
½ cup chopped walnuts
½ cup water
½ cup whole wheat flour
½ teaspoon ground cinnamon
1 teaspoon vanilla extract
1/3 cup vegetable oil
2 ½ cups dry pancake mix
2 tablespoons milk

Preheat oven to 250 degrees. Preheat waffle iron. In a bowl, mix the pancake mix and whole wheat flour. Form a well in the center, and pour in water, oil, and syrup. Stir until evenly moist. Stir in the milk, vanilla, and cinnamon. Fold in walnuts. Pour about 1/3 cup batter per waffle into the waffle iron, and cook 5 minutes, until done. Transfer waffles to a baking dish, and place in the preheated oven. Cook 5 minutes, or until crisp. #Delish!

World's Easiest Waffle Sticks

⅓ cup canola oil
½ teaspoon of salt
1 teaspoon baking powder
1 teaspoon baking soda
1¾ cups all-purpose flour
2 cups buttermilk
2 eggs

Preheat waffle maker according to the manufacturer's instructions. Mix all ingredients together. Ladle batter onto waffle iron cooking surface. Bake until desired brownness is reached. Serve immediately. #Delish!

Yummy Yeast Raised Waffles

¼ teaspoon salt
½ cup melted butter
1 (.25 ounce) package active dry yeast
1 tablespoon white sugar
1 teaspoon vanilla extract
2 ½ cups sifted all-purpose flour
2 cups warm milk
4 egg whites
4 egg yolks

In a small bowl, dissolve yeast in warm milk. Let stand until creamy, about 10 minutes. In a large bowl, mix the flour, salt, and sugar. Beat the egg yolks into the yeast mixture, and mix into the dry ingredients. Stir in the vanilla extract and melted butter. In a large glass or metal bowl, whip egg whites until stiff peaks form. Carefully fold into the waffle batter. Let stand in a warm place about 45 minutes, or until doubled in size. Preheat a Belgian-style waffle iron, and coat with cooking spray. Place ¾ to 1 cup of batter onto the hot iron; close the lid. Cook until the steaming subsides and the waffle is golden brown. #Delish!

BONUS:

Blueberry Maple Syrup
1 cup pure maple syrup
1½ cups fresh blueberries
Pinch kosher salt
Pinch orange zest (optional)
Put all ingredients in a small saucepan set over medium heat. Bring to a boil and then reduce heat to maintain a strong simmer to allow the mixture to thicken slightly, about 5 minutes. Strain, if desired, and serve. Makes about 2 cups (1½ cups if strained). #Delish!

Homemade Honey Butter
1 teaspoon vanilla extract
3 ounces (1/4 cup) honey
8 ounces unsalted butter
Pinch of salt
Using a stand mixer fitted with the whisk attachment or a handheld mixer, beat unsalted butter (softened) until very light and fluffy, about 3 minutes. With the mixer running, add honey in a slow and steady stream. Continue to beat to incorporate the honey, about 1 minute longer, scraping down the sides of the bowl as needed. Beat in salt and vanilla extract. Use the butter at room temperature. #Delish!

Thank you for your purchase!
May you enjoy and be well!

ABOUT THE AUTHOR

I am a Tennessee native and a connoisseur of good eats. My culinary delights are inspired by my Southern roots.

I am from cornbread and cabbage, fried chicken and Kool-Aid soaked lemon slices.

I am from hen houses, persimmon trees and juicy, red tomatoes on the vine.

I am from sunflowers growing wild in summer and homemade ice cream in the winter.

I am from family reunions, blue collar men, happy housewives, and Sunday dinners.

I am from spiritual folks who didn't always get it right, but believed in the power of prayer – and taught it to their kids.

I am from the hottest of hot summers and kids running barefoot and free through thirsty Tennessee grass.

I am from a grandmother who sang gospel that was magic…song drenched air would tumble from her lungs, leap into your spirit and make you feel fantastic things.

I am from hard, heartfelt lessons about living and kitchens full of the perfume of love.

♥♥♥ *This book is from my heart to yours.* ♥♥♥

For info, freebies & new book notices, follow @SoDelishDish on social media!
Scan with your smartphone!

FIND MORE BOOKS ONLINE

Printed in Great Britain
by Amazon